THE ART AND SCIENCE OF LEADERSHIP & MANAGEMENT

CENTURIES OF BEST PRACTICES THAT CREATE A POSITIVE CULTURE FOR GROWTH

FRITZ GRUPE

"*We are what we repeatedly do. Excellence, then, is not an act, but a habit.*"

— ARISTOTLE

CONTENTS

INTRODUCTION

THE EFFECTIVE LEADER

Leaders and managers are chosen by others.

Ever wonder how and why were they picked? What are the skillsets and choices they made that demonstrated they were the right ones to lead, manage, and call the shots?

The following is an outline of some of the skillsets behind the choices that I, my CEO friends from great growth companies, and business school leaders consider best practices.

This booklet isn't a "How-To"; it's more like your pilot's pre-flight checklist. These are timeless principles recognized for centuries by myself, top producers, and leaders.

If you're searching to take a deeper dive into these concepts, check out my book, "Enjoy the Ride," where I go all-in on these principles, complete with anecdotes from my own business journey.

CHANGE, INNOVATION, AND COMPETITION

*P*rior to his death in 1882, Charles Darwin said, "It is not the strongest or most intelligent that survive, it is the most adaptive."

Change is inevitable and necessary.

View it as your friend, embrace it, manage it, or it will manage you. As Jack Welch said, "If the world, your competitors are changing faster than you – the end is in sight."

In approaching change, study the obstacle or challenge in light of the mission. Why is it a problem? Whose problem is it? What can realistically be done to solve it? Be alert to not falling into the despair or the victim trap. Embrace new directions and solutions—and establish clear and measurable goals.

Sometimes, despite your best efforts, adversity can catch you unaware. You can prepare for the unforeseen (i.e. a recession), but the *Unforeseen-Unforeseen*, something not even on your radar, can potentially destroy even successful management teams and organizations.

Management must never become complacent. Strong

managers must continuously build and nurture their teams, giving them greater resilience to face these unexpected challenges.

Einstein said, "Education should start at birth and end only at death." Continue to sharpen your saw. Learn your organization through and through. Spend the time to discover your team's strengths and weaknesses. As Drucker said, "A manager's job is to build on people's strengths and make their weaknesses irrelevant."

A manager always has limited resources, time, human capital, and financial capital. Continuous preparation is the key to making the best use of them.

Preparedness decreases surprises!

CHARACTER, CULTURE, VALUES

a great organization isn't built on skillsets or techniques; it's founded on the *core character and values* of its leaders. This is the DNA that sets the tone for the company culture and even carves out its brand identity.

Before you fixate on the 'how,' dig deep into the 'who' and 'why.' If you are on the wrong path, getting there faster or more efficiently is of little value.

Place priority on integrity, honesty, humility, and patience. The Golden Rule is a good start. Strive for excellence and have pride in your work. Customers and future generations will thank you.

Ask yourself: what do you hope people say about you at your funeral? Then build backward from there.

TRUST

Trust is essential. I repeat: *trust is essential.* What is more important than trust in a relationship?

Keep your word. Don't break promises, especially to yourself.

Learn to forgive yourself as well as others. Everyone makes mistakes, that is where we learn.

MAKING DECISIONS AND
ASSESSING RISKS

*W*hen there is a perplexing problem to solve, first decide if the problem is a lack of information (data) or the people in charge.

When you must choose between two bad choices, have the mental discipline and clear thinking to find the best solution.

Understand the concept of *opportunity costs* that affects the outcome of all your decisions, both personal and business.

Most people think of opportunity cost only from the "where to invest" point of view and forget to analyze their current portfolio, not only from ROI but time allocated.

I hired my first gardener at twenty-four. Why would I work for minimum wage when I could pay for a year of gardening with one house sale? Gardening for enjoyment is different.

Not everything that can be fixed is *worth* fixing once the opportunity cost is considered. An entity that makes a small return can consume a lot of energy. This can be a challenge for those of us who want to stick things out.

Tenacity is a necessary quality in life and business, but when you hang on too long to an idea, project, or person to the detriment of your overall goal, that same quality can become a weakness.

I'll outline a few considerations below. For more on *pulling the pin*, i.e. making the hard choice, see my book *Enjoy the Ride*.

Tips for making hard decisions:

- Set a deadline.
- Lean on research.
- Turn to the experts.
- Be honest about any indecisiveness.
- Listen to your intuition.
- Focus on the reward of taking action.

Choosing A Partner

I often advise investors that choosing a managing partner is more important than the details of a deal. Look beyond the economics and be sure you're going into business with someone who will be able to fix problems as they come along.

GOALS, PLANNING, EXECUTION, AND RESULTS

*D*reams and aspirations are essential, but they are not goals. *Goals define how you measure success.* What you measure improves.

Ask yourself: did today advance my long-term goals? Stay focused on your goals, no mission creep, but keep your peripheral vision. Always look for how to do things better and be alert to new ideas. We'll get to rules for goal setting and the reason people do not set goals in a bit.

What you think is possible for you to accomplish is key. We cannot exceed what we view as reality. Whether you think you can or whether you think you can't, you're right!

Our performance follows the image we have of ourselves. Therefore, when you change your beliefs, your performance will follow. You automatically move toward the picture you have of yourself.

Creative people focus on the results they want to produce as if they currently exist! Think about it, the future is now as soon as you can visualize it and have a plan to get there. Creative people take more risks, perform forward planning, and have a personality that looks at obstacles as opportunities. *Opportunities are often cleverly disguised as obstacles or challenges.*

A vision is great, even necessary, so the big question is, do you have the courage and ability to execute it? A vision without the ability to execute it has no value.

WHEN ERNEST GALLO, a self-made titan in the wine industry, was asked how he pulled off the 'impossible,' his response was illuminating: "I did not. I accomplished the obvious." Ever notice that when an amateur fails, he missed the subtleties; when a pro fails, he missed the obvious? No matter your level of mastery or accomplishment, it's important to keep your peripheral vision.

A smaller version of a dream: from age 23 until 26, I was a house salesman. At 27, I wanted to start building houses, but I had no contractor license, so I hired a back-of-the-pick-up contractor. At 28, I started planning my first Master Planned Community (a 10-year plan with 4,000 homes and a shopping center). I had no capital of my own to invest. This plan included the first man-made lakes in Northern California, the first underground utilities, the first cable TV in San Joaquin County, the first attached housing in Stockton, the largest covered slip marina in Northern California, had the most expensive homes in Stockton, and the least expensive new homes ($15,995). Twenty years later, the city named a park after me, and I was listed in Builder Magazine as one of the USA housing giants, ranked #28 in the nation. I provide an in-depth look at how I accomplished this in my book, *Enjoy The Ride.*

GOALS

Let's look at the components of a goal.

- It must be in writing, or it's a dream.
- Clear in scope and intent.
- Have a timeframe.
- If it's a big goal, broken down into bite-size. (Eating an elephant.)
- Consider cost/benefit.
- Change with new data. (Remember, if the outside world is changing faster than you, the end is inevitable.)
- Share with someone you trust, and the chances of success will increase.

It's worth saying again: a goal you can't figure out how to accomplish is an aspiration, not a goal!

WHY GOALS?

How else are you going to get where you want to go? In the wise words of Charlie Brown, "How can I be lost when I don't know where I am going?" In other words, if you don't know where you are going, any road will get you there—and the converse is also true.

WHY DON'T PEOPLE MAKE GOALS?

- Fear of failure
- Don't like accountability.

- Don't know where to start.

If you aren't sure where to start, make a list of your aspirations and see how they match your strengths and weaknesses. We all have them!

A manager's job, whether it is for yourself or your company, is to build on a person's strengths and make their weaknesses irrelevant. Setting goals is a valuable tool in that process.

LEADERSHIP AND MANAGEMENT

*G*reat leaders and managers have at least four things in common: they all have fire in the belly, they are hardworking, disciplined, and committed to their mission.

Often, there are differences between great leaders and great managers.

ENTREPRENEURS AND LEADERS tend to be curious people with a vision focused on maximizing opportunities. They're dedicated to the mission, so much so that personal gains take a back seat. Their passion and the clarity of their strategy are magnetic; others see it and want in. They want to become part of something larger that promises to make a difference. That's the kind of pull that turns a mission into a collective triumph.

A clear vision, mission, and strategy are vital, but they're only part of the equation. Big wins don't happen without the boots-on-the-ground folks who turn ideas into action. You need implementers and problem-solvers in the mix, or else the vision stays just that—a vision. You need an entire band to make great music. At the end of the day, *a vision is only as good as your ability to execute.*

NOW, LET'S LOOK AT THE ORGANIZATIONAL LEADER, THE MANAGER.

Organizations have a system, a logic, of their own. Embedded in history, they are weighted in tradition, corporate culture, and inertia. Managers are generally rational and systematic. At times, they might let the attraction of the tried-and-true path preempt the challenge of taking risks and striking out in new directions. These executives get ahead by managing risk. They direct and control, often adopting impersonal attitudes toward goals, which rise out of necessity rather than from a desire or vision. They view their work as an enabling, incremental process. In fact, they may get punished for bold failure; therefore, they dislike ambiguity and prefer certainty.

A technologically oriented and economically successful society and/or organization often depreciates the value of great leaders. It holds a deep faith in traditional methods for solving problems, focusing on *managing* instead of *imagining.*

What elevates a manager from good to great? Great managers get things done and have a 'go for it attitude.' They recognize that *perfection is the enemy of progress.* They do not kick the can down the road. A half-ass attempt now is better than a perfect attempt never!

Pretend you are standing on a cliff. With the right answer, you stay. With the wrong answer, you're pushed over. But with *no* answer, you're pushed over, too. *Great managers make decisions and manage the consequences.*

So, WHICH IS BETTER, the charismatic leader or the tried and true manager? Are they in conflict?

Although there may be differences, I do not think they conflict. Senior execs focus on managing risk; entrepreneurs focus on maximizing opportunity. I believe we need *both*.

The wise leader and manager surround themselves with people possessing different talents, especially strengths differing from their own.

Regardless of whether you align yourself more with the leader type or the manager type, it's clear both are essential. Remember the old saying: if you want to go fast, go alone; if you want to go far, go together.

And of course, it goes without saying that *it's critical to have a clear mission that is communicated throughout the organization.*

ADDITIONAL THOUGHTS

MANAGEMENT BY WALKING AROUND. There's no better way to get to know your products and people. Be a visible part of your organization and have stand-up meetings. This will help you learn the value and if it's working - decentralization. You need this system to foster growth, increase creativity, and manage change at the lowest practical level. See Jim Morgan's book, *Applied Wisdom: Bad News Is Good News If You Do Something About It*, for more.

. . .

TAKE OWNERSHIP OF THE TASK. Who owns the monkey (i.e. whose problem is it)? Feed or kill the monkey, don't starve it to death. Either fix it, give it to someone else, but never ignore it.

WHEN I WAS CEO, I had a saying, "For every challenge facing The Grupe Company, there will be a name attached and that name will never be Fritz Grupe." (i.e., everyone should try to work out of the job.)

HAVING SAID THAT, *delegation is not abdication.*

I LIKE PERFORMANCE STANDARDS, but they are not goals. They are activities a person does. They clarify job descriptions and give subordinates more freedom to act. The boss should be advised of non-performance, so no news is good news. Performance standards ensure that there are measurable goals that, if unmet, can signal issues before they become larger problems. For more on this, take a look at the article I wrote in section 10, Additional Resources.

PEOPLE ARE YOUR MAIN ASSET. Protect them! Learn to be a better coach – practice Pygmalion (see in people what they may not see in themselves).

. . .

PRAISE BEHAVIOR THAT WORKS. When behavior is not up to expectations, don't put more doubts in their mind. Instead, remind them of the way they normally do it correctly, i.e., "As good as you are, this is the way you normally catch the ball."

SELF-ASSESSMENT AND REFLECTION

*L*et's get real: If you're a leader or manager, you've got to come to terms with the fact that life isn't always fair.

Sometimes, good people get dealt bad hands.

Sound familiar? Well, it should. Even the Bible tells us life's not going to be easy. The key is to play your own hand as best as you can, instead of envying (coveting) the cards someone else was dealt and wishing it was your hand.

In leadership, as in life, you have to roll with the punches and make the most of what you've got.

Remember, what one person sees as an obstacle, another sees as an opportunity. Think about this for a moment: The magnitude of any problem is determined by your perception of the problem. Put another way, how you *see* the problem may *be* the problem!

When you make a mistake, do you see yourself as a failure or that you just had a learning experience? If you feel like a failure, you are much less likely to try another new idea.

Ben Franklin said, "Thinking is difficult. That's why so

few people engage in it." Most people won't reexamine their fundamental assumptions and beliefs, but what if there are better ideas out there?

Focus on what you can control. Don't let circumstances or other people determine who you are or what you can be! Why turn control of your life over to someone or something else?

Have courage! Attitude is key. Take control and accept responsibility. If attitude affects your performance, what affects your attitude?

Attitude and confidence are byproducts of the basics:

1. How do you feel about yourself (you are your only real critic)?
2. Are you proud of who you are and what you have done based on the opportunities you have been presented and what you have to work with?
3. Do you like the way you look?
4. Do you dress appropriately?
5. Do you practice good posture?
6. Do you feel fit?
7. Do you allow time for self-renewal – meditation?
8. Be prepared – get rid of fear.
9. Are you stressed out?
10. Do you have realistic expectations? Are you meeting your goals?
11. Do you really comprehend what is going on around you – listen, learn, and understand?
12. Do you support others? If so, they will be there for you.
13. Do you allow for joy in your life?
14. Do you practice—and express—gratitude?

· · ·

RELATIONSHIPS ARE essential in order to maximize joy in life. The value of a friend cannot be overemphasized for mutual support in times of stress and confusion.

Studies show what people with joy in their lives have in common. They all have a sense of purpose, value relationships, are fun to be with, practice gratitude, prioritize health, don't play victim, and realize success is seldom permanent, nor is failure. They also happen to be the most productive and understand the difference between achieving and achievement.

Achievement is temporary.

Achieving brings lasting joy.

SELF MANAGEMENT IN DIFFICULT TIMES

There is the misconception that there is not enough time in the day.

Actually, there is the perfect amount. If you had more, you would just add more things to what you didn't get done since there is an endless supply of new problems and opportunities with new ideas to explore.

The answer to a perceived shortage of time is to prioritize.

1. Focus on important – not urgent
2. Use of a To Do sheet (example attached)
3. Get rid of anything that is not useful

Luck happens when preparedness meets opportunity. A detailed five-year plan with goals and a full recognition of your strengths and weaknesses increases the chance of success. Charlie Brown said, "How can I be lost when I don't know where I am going?"

Knowing where you want to go is the first step in getting there.

BE PREPARED for threats and cycles, as well as opportunities.

The best organizations know bad things can happen periodically. Circumstances do change, but values don't. Have a Plan B, Protect downside, however, don't compromise your principles. There are certain things you can comprise, but certain things you can't.

Mission creep is not good, but without peripheral vision, you will miss out on a changing world.

Anticipate problems – don't wait for them to surprise you. Be able to play the hand you are dealt.

Cash is king. Warren Buffet said he had seven big deals in his whole business career that made him the financial winner he is today. Lots of good ones, a few losers, but seven were big.

Tenacity is essential for an entrepreneur, leader, or manager. So, with that as a given, when do you stop doing something you really had your heart set on doing?

This is when to consider *opportunity costs* and weigh whether to *pull the pin*.

DEALING WITH FEAR

Simple to state but hard to do.

When dealing with fear, take a hard look at opportunity costs. For a closer look at this critically important concept, see my book, *Enjoy the Ride,* with personal examples. Your greatest strength can be your biggest weakness.

Faith and fear are polar opposites, but they share one characteristic: they both want you to believe in something that has not yet happened!

Fear can be overcome by being prepared, doing your homework and having a clear plan for success.

Anxious, yes! Fear, no!

In dealing with stress, first understand the cause, then stop or mitigate it. Use solutions I suggested in this publication, details in my book *Enjoy the Ride* – i.e., time for self-renewal, meditation, time management, prioritization, perception of the problems, and practice what brings joy.

A FINAL THOUGHT

As I mentioned previously, successful leaders and managers have several similar strengths: hardworking, tenacious, and focused. So why do they occasionally fail or get replaced by a competitor?

Often, it comes down to a lack of peripheral vision and a focus on daily goals to the exclusion of seeing the long game. However, business is infinite, not finite. Perfecting the details and excelling in day-to-day operations won't save you if you've missed the obvious.

Be aware of transformative shifts in the world of commerce. Stay adaptable and keep improving. Darwin captured this idea over one hundred years ago in a sentence, "It's not the strongest or most intelligent that survive, but the most adaptable."

Besides, in the end, the joy comes from achieving, not achievement.

STRATEGY

BRANDING, POSITIONING, DIFFERENTIATION

*P*eter Drucker, described as the "Founder of Modern Management," invented management by objectives, which allows for the ability for managers to have more independence and freedom to take action and make decisions.

According to Drucker, the first questions for an organization are:

- What is our business?
- Who is our customer?
- What does the customer consider value?

This may seem basic, but I have been surprised at how many organizations do not have a clear answer to these questions.

For example, in 2000, I was the first chair of the Foundation Advisory Board for the new University of California campus to be built in Merced, the tenth in the system, which opened in 2005.

The new Chancellor was Carol Tomlinson Keasey, Professor of Social Sciences and Dean at UC Davis. While well qualified to find new deans and vice presidents for the new campus, Keasey had no background in reading blueprints, developing land, building infrastructure, or marketing.

I spent a lot of time trying to help her with this great challenge. One of my early questions once she had hired a leadership team was: How do you think the new UC campus will be perceived by the future student population? They have a vision of UC Berkley, Davis, Santa Cruz, etc. They are all different. What is your vision for Merced? How will a new campus in the middle of nowhere in the Central Valley be perceived? Who will be your customer?

She had never thought about the new campus that way, so I suggested a great consultant for this job, Jack Trout, whom I agreed to pay. She agreed, so I hosted an offsite retreat in Stockton at a country club I had built.

By noon on the first day, her Provost, Deans and Vice Presidents could not agree on who the customer was! Was it the students, the parents, the professors, who?

You cannot develop a market plan or decide how to differentiate your product without agreeing on the customer.

It was finally decided by her team that it was to be the professors. Now here is a business school subject for debate!

Drucker has another quote, "Only two things are important in a company: marketing and innovation, everything else is a cost."

I learned this at 28 years old starting my first Master Planned Community. How do you create urgency for a home when you have room to build 4,000 of them?

For more on this subject, see my book, *Enjoy the Ride,* or Jack Trout's *Differentiate or Die.*

TEAM BUILDING

HIRING, MANAGEMENT, PERFORMANCE STANDARDS

*O*ne cannot be a great team player without helping the rest of the team. In other words, to *be* the MVP, you have to help everyone on your team *also* be MVP's.

To do this, you must be aware of what and where everybody is, how they are doing, and respect their different talents.

As I've said before: *Trust is essential.*

Teams are made up of humans with different attributes and challenges. Sooner or later everyone can use a little help.

People help people who help them move the team forward. Conversely, those who do not help are left alone when they have a problem.

Everyone in an organization must share the values and mission or they belong on another team. Let's take a look at the characteristics of a good team.

. . .

SUCCESSFUL TEAMS:

- Are focused
- Have faith in the purpose and mission
- Have courage, are hardworking and determined
- Care about others on the team and support them
- Are humble listeners or encouraging coaches when needed
- Respect and trust each other
- Have freedom and authority to act and be creative
- And, for sure, have fun!

ADDITIONAL THOUGHTS

Following are a few more key points that can help you nurture a stronger team.

IN BRAINSTORMING, there are no bad ideas, but once a plan has been agreed upon, there must be alignment. Everyone tries their best to make the play work.

VECTOR OF POWER EXAMPLE – 5 units going the same direction. If two start pulling in opposite directions, now what is THE NET power forward? (Answer: one. The two going in the opposite direction cancel out two going in the same direction. Therefore, there is a net one. Going in exactly the opposite direction is rare, but deviation off the main thrust is common.) For more on this, see my book, *Enjoy the Ride.*

. . .

How do you select a team to fulfill the vision, mission and purpose? First, you must answer Peter Drucker's three premises above, then pick the team with the skill set and personality to do that. A really big important job!

Who do you hire, and what is the best process for successful hiring?

Dr. Pierre Mornell, the author of "Hiring Smart," was a consultant and friend who did a survey of 100 companies, many from the Bay Area who were in my Young Presidents' Organization (YPO) Chapter.

Mornell tackled the question: "What is the cost of a bad hire?"

The answer is: way more than their direct pay while they are employed! It's lost time, lost customers, and decreased morale in the organization. People lose confidence in leadership when the wrong people are hired to fill a position.

Of the 100 companies in the survey, the average cost of a bad hire in the late 1990s was slightly over $1 million and took 1 ½ years to remedy! That's a lot!

In 1985, I made a plaque for our executives, "Businesses don't compete, their managers do."

SUPPORTING GUIDELINES AND PRINCIPLES

*C*onsider this: If your job has purpose and brings you joy, why would you want to stop doing it? If it does not, why are you doing it?

Let's look at a few more ideas to add to your leadership and managerial toolbox.

IMPROVE YOUR LISTENING SKILLS.

Practice on your teenager. Before you can fix a problem, you must understand it. Listen – Learn – Act. The reverse is painful. If you first don't agree on the data, better communication does not help.

As my friend Jim Morgan said, "Bad news is good news if you do something about it." And as Henry Ford said, "Don't find fault, find a remedy."

Improving your listening skills will improve your negotiating skills. This creates a win-win.

. . .

YOU HAVE a problem when the process becomes an end in itself. Think of many government agencies. The question I have for them is, "Do you consider yourself a cop or a facilitator?" Those who consider themselves facilitators are the ones who make life pleasant for those they serve. Public service should be a noble endeavor.

NO AGENDA, no meeting—*know your objective!*—and must leave with an action plan.

IF YOU DON'T LIKE what you attract, examine what you radiate.

IN JUDGING PERFORMANCE, know the difference between brains and a bull market.

WHEN REQUIRED to be judgmental regarding another human being, proceed with caution! "How can you think of saying, 'Friend let me help you get rid of that speck in your eye,' when you can't see the log in your own." Luke 6:42

PASSION DOES NOT REQUIRE an emotional response. Becoming overemotional can affect logic. Conviction and control can coexist.

FOCUS ON HEALTH SPAN, not life span.

. . .

ADVENTURE CREATES A NEED FOR INTERDEPENDENCE.

BE CAREFUL OF A ONE-TRICK PONY, or it better be a hell of a trick.

GOOD IDEAS that you can implement are harder to find than the capital it takes to do them.

THE EASIEST TIME TO correct a problem is just before it happens. Learn to anticipate problems before they occur. I learned from training dogs and horses.

IN REAL ESTATE MATTERS, as in most businesses, you make your profit when you buy, not when you sell. My friend, Jim Morgan, says, "Bought right ½ sold." This does not mean it is not extremely important for management to increase value. It is essential; it's just very hard to fix a bad buy. In real estate, you cannot fix a bad location but can fix bad management or repurpose the asset.

LIFE IS NEVER in perfect balance. Learn to live an integrated life, striving for balance.

HUMOR IS ESSENTIAL.

. . .

WE OFTEN HEAR people talk about the world's problems, but talking alone doesn't create change. If you want to make a real difference, the key is to start local. Get involved in your local community through volunteering or local politics. Taking action is how you'll make an impact and spur genuine change. As you sow, so shall ye reap. I was a founder of five 501c3's in San Joaquin County that have been very successful and are well funded because they are producing good results that can and are being measured.

PRACTICE DEFERRED CONSUMPTION. Never spend more than you make, invest in your future. When asked, "What is the most important mathematical formula?" Einstein said, "Compounding." Know the Rule of 72 - If you want to double your money and you make 6% per year, divide 6 into 72, answer 12 years, at 10% it's 7.2 years or the reverse, if want to double your money every 10 years, it takes 7.2% return.

OFFSITE TEAM BUILDING can be very productive, sometimes with spouses; this is a great time to recognize their importance.

LEAN ON OTHERS. Mentors, advisors, and consultants have been essential to my career. I have been fortunate to have some of the best, recognized throughout the USA, heads of major corporations. department heads of major universities (i.e., Cal & Stanford). Experienced people may not always know the right answers but can spot the wrong ones – the value of a sanity check.

TRADITIONS HAVE A ROLE. Tying back to our history provides perspective and appreciation, which brings joy.

FOCUS IS ESSENTIAL, but don't lose peripheral vision.

LEAD BY EXAMPLE. If only the janitor or owner picks up the trash, you've got a lack of teamwork in the organization. No one should be above helping somebody else.

PREDATORS AND COMPETITORS play a positive role in our ecosystem.

WANT A PROMOTION? Don't delegate up.

YOU CANNOT HIDE a winner any more than you can hide a loser.

YOU JUDGE yourself by your intent. Others judge you by your actions.

· · ·

GUT FEEL, a woman's intuition if you will, needs to be used, especially when it comes to people.

MANY SOLUTIONS for today's challenges require adaptive coalitions. See Steve Case's book, *The Third Wave*.

IF YOU CANNOT COMPROMISE, don't get into politics—and for sure don't get married. - *Senator Alan Simpson*

A FINAL THOUGHT, in the words of Thomas Jefferson: "It is neither wealth, nor splendor, but tranquility and occupation, which give happiness."

WHILE YOU ARE WAITING for your dreams to materialize, life happens, so enjoy the ride.

ADDITIONAL RESOURCES

*I*f you're interested in delving more deeply into any of the concepts mentioned in this handbook, they are covered in my book. For easy reference, here's a look at what you'll find.

"ENJOY THE RIDE" CHAPTERS

Chapter 1 - Daring to Dream

Chapter 2 - Values Worth Their Value

Chapter 3 - Learning Financial Responsibility

Chapter 4 - Getting Curious: Learn to Ask the Right Questions

Chapter 5 - Becoming a Lifelong Learner

Chapter 6 - Listening and Communicating Effectively

Chapter 7 - Having the Courage to Take Action

Chapter 8 - Building Confidence and Trust Through Action

Chapter 9 - Practicing Patience

I WROTE the following article for the Grupe Company newsletter, published in Spring 1985. I believe it touches on important concepts relevant to leadership and management.

OBSERVATIONS
by Greenlaw "Fritz" Grupe, Jr., Chairman/CEO

STANDARDS OF PERFORMANCE: Who needs them?! Who reads them? They sound too business school-ish. Not practical. Sounds like an idea my boss came home with after attending a conference; the idea will soon fade. Who has time to set them when there is so much work to be done? It sure doesn't sound entrepreneurial.

These are all statements that I've heard when people discuss the value of setting standards of performance. My 25 years of experience in the business world have led me to believe that performance standards are a timesaving device. They allow managers more freedom to act, more control of their own destiny, and a happier boss/subordinate relationship. I have found that they stimulate creative thinking, help formulate the company's objectives, improve the basis for budgeting, and greatly enhance communication, not only between boss and subordinate, but among peers.

We all know that bosses are far from the textbook great managers. They can sometimes be un realistic, emotional or capricious; but with the proper setting of performance standards, much of this mis-communication between boss and subordinate will disappear.

As a boss was overheard saying, "I'm not trying to evaluate your performance. I'm just trying to locate it. Please show me some footprints in the sand."

That leads to the old adage, "What your boss doesn't know you're doing, you're not doing." If a person doesn't know what is important, he can focus on the unimportant. When the day of judgement comes, there can be great discrepancies as to how well a person has performed his job.

In any conversation I've had with a manager, when I have asked him how he knows if he's doing a good job, he has an opinion. It is interesting to note if it's the same as mine. Therefore, I think there is a strong case for a subordinate asking his boss for the opportunity to set performance standards.

Now, how does a boss go about doing this? First, he doesn't impose standards. The standards are set by the subordinate and given to the boss for approval.

Once the boss has approved those standards, then the subordinate has the total freedom to act within them. The subordinate should agree that he will always bring to his boss's attention an adverse trend in his own performance before a failure point is reached. If he can fix it, he should. If he doesn't know what to do, then he should talk to the boss (i.e., No news is good news.).

At review periods there should be few surprises. (Remember, in starting to set these performance standards, an imperfect standard is better than none at all. Through time they will be perfected. I have an old saying: "A half-assed action now is better than a perfect action never.")

When the boss goes home at night or on the weekend, he should feel comfortable knowing that things are going as per agreement. Otherwise, he either has an incompetent person or an insubordinate one.

I have found that it is very helpful for the boss to set his performance standards first and to give them out to everyone who reports to him before he asks them to do theirs. This way, there is a clear understanding of what the boss thinks his job is and how he is to be judged on his performance.

Performance standards are not goals. They are activities that a person does. In setting them, there is not a grade of A, B or C. It is a pass/fail situation, i.e., when the subordinate sets the standard, he agrees that he will not fall below that standard without immediately bringing it to his boss's attention. Performance standards are arrived at subjectively and expressed quantitatively so that performance can be evaluated objectively. I have found that an easy way to start is to ask somebody to list the five or ten key things that he's responsible to do, just list them as an activity, in one sentence, if possible. Then in a couple of sentences, ask him to explain why he does this activity, its purpose. From there, the subordinate can set standards with regard to quantity (i.e., the existence of a plan); quality (deviation, acceptance, or rejection); timeliness (when this is supposed to be done) and cost (dollar or time commitment the activity requires). Brevity, clear scope and intent, and measurability are the key factors. A person first setting his performance standards may spend several hours on them himself and a few hours with his boss to communicate and agree on them; however, once this is done, they give him freedom to act throughout the year or years. When an activity changes, a person can drop it; or, as he wants to add new activities, he can come to his boss indicating what he wants to do and what the standards are. That way, the boss must buy into the subordinate's program of development. Results should be a clear understanding between the boss and the subordinate as to what is going to happen between now and the next review period.

We have used performance standards at The Grupe Company for a decade. I have found that as managers slack off in getting their standards of performance done, they have paid the price in lack of communication at a later date. That is more time-consuming than if everybody had taken the time to agree on standards of performance in the beginning. Therefore, I find this process to be a great timesaving device that allows boss and subordinate wider freedom to act. Consequently, both look forward much more to the review period.

PERFORMANCE STANDARDS WORKSHEET

Name:
Title:
Approved By:

ACTIVITY - A job I do.

PURPOSE - Why I do a job.

STANDARDS - How I know I am doing it acceptably.

1. QUANTITY - Existence of a written plan.
2. QUALITY - Deviation, Acceptance, Rejection
3. TIMELINES
4. ECONOMICS

TO DO

URGENT:

   (RANK A, B, OR C)

TO SEE OR CALL:

CONTINUING ATTENTION:

AWAITING DEVELOPMENT:

ABOUT THE AUTHOR

Greenlaw "Fritz" Grupe, Jr. is chairman and founder of the Grupe Company of Stockton, California. Since 1966, it has created twenty-three master-planned communities in ten states, 14,000 apartments, and developed in excess of seven million square feet of office, commercial, and storage space.

A graduate of the University of California, Berkeley, Grupe is a past president of the Urban Land Institute, past chairman of the Northern California and Golden Gate Chapters of the Young Presidents' Organization, and he has been inducted into the distinguished California Home-building Foundation's Hall of Fame.

He is a large California agriculturalist, growing wine grapes, apples, cherries, olives, and walnuts and raising cattle. For twenty years, he was an international competitor in the equestrian sport of Combined Driving. Taking up the sport at the age of sixty, he became the first person to claim the United States Equestrian Federation's National Championship title for both Single and Pairs Driving. Fritz and Phyllis, his wife of over sixty years, have four children, twenty grandchildren, and eight great-grandchildren.